What Can a Bird See?

by John Serrano

A bird can see houses.

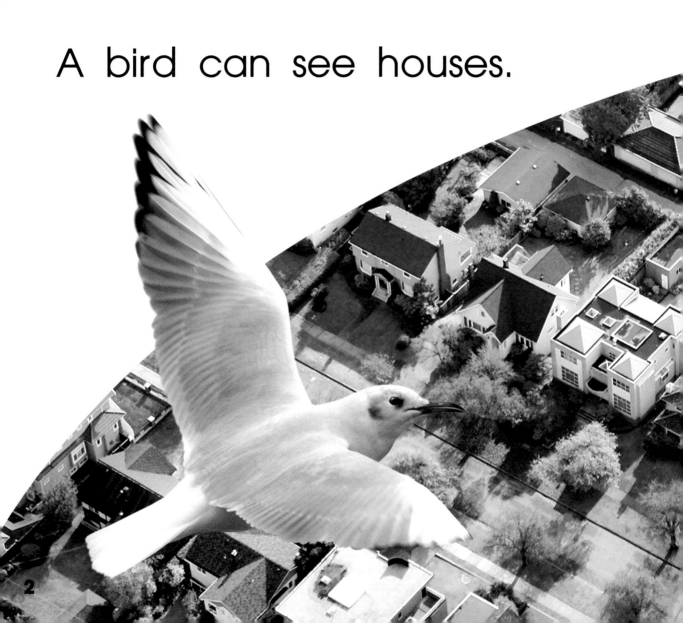

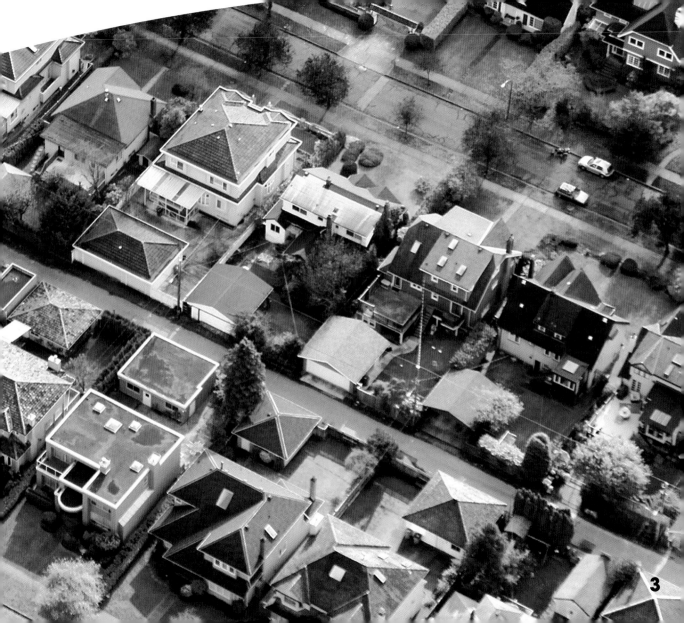

A bird can see trees.

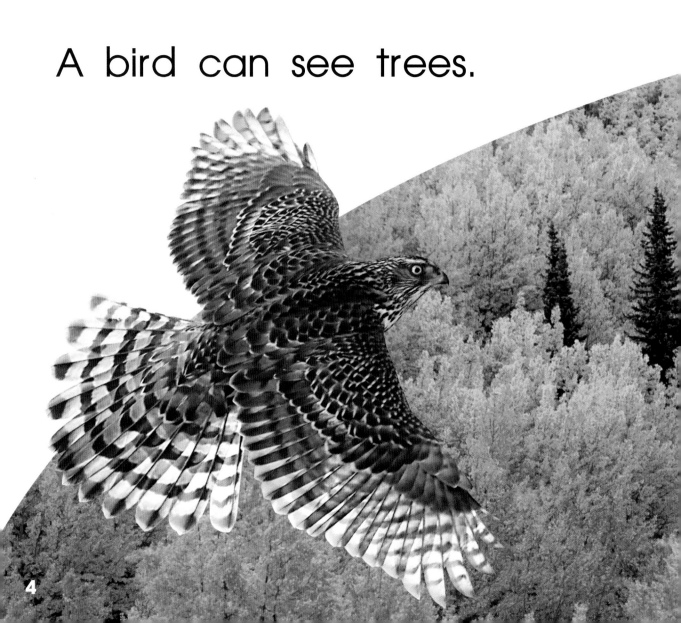

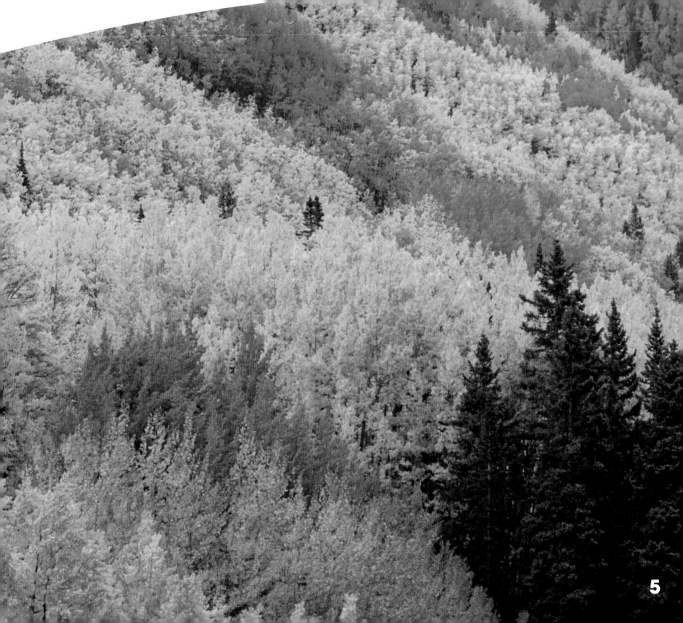

A bird can see streets.

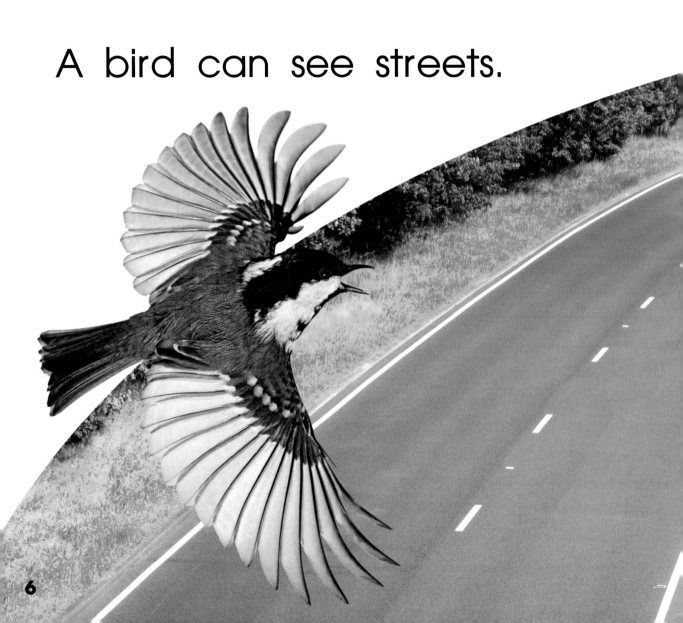

A bird can see fields.

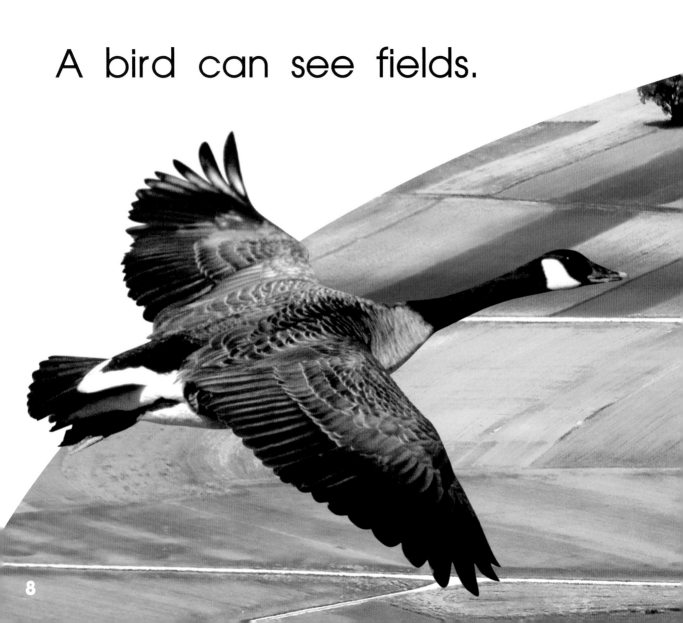

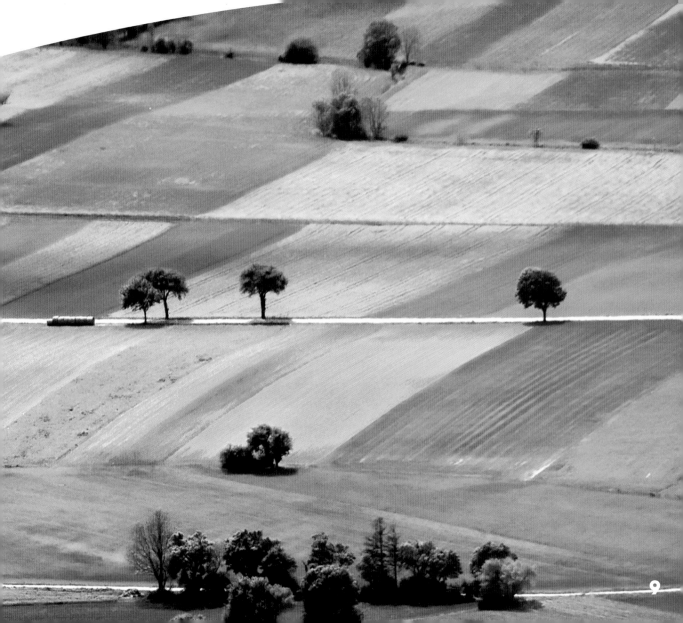

A bird can see mountains.

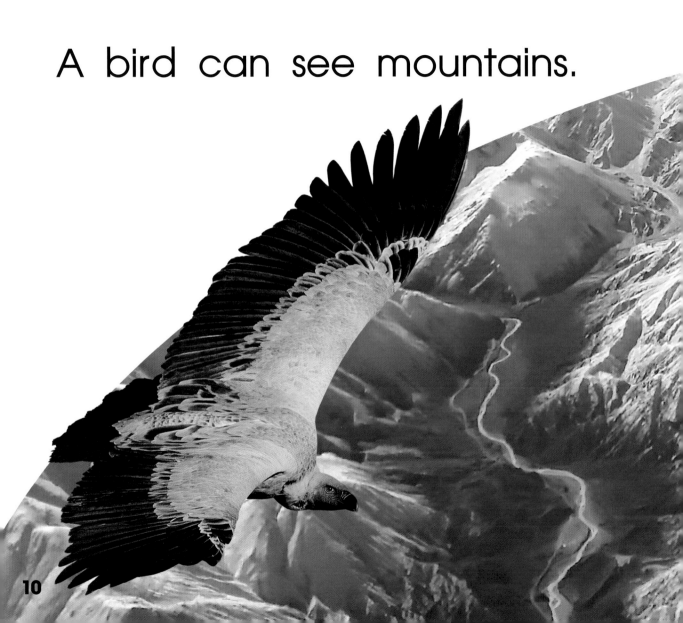

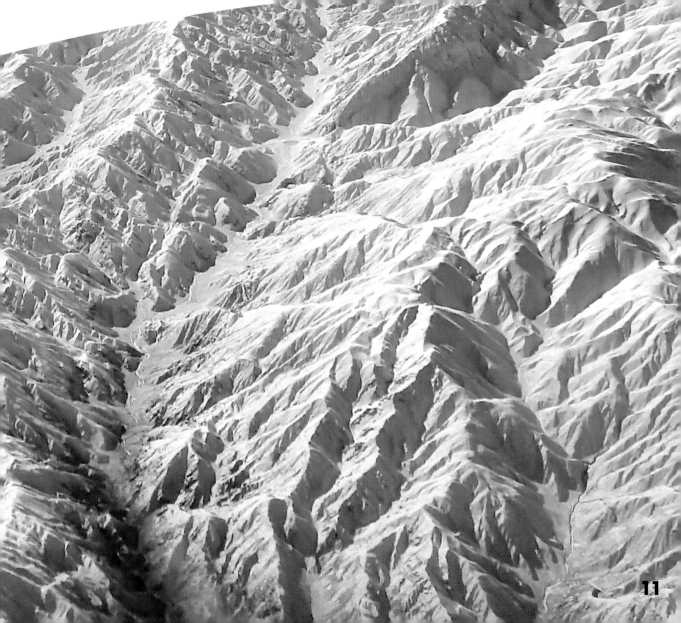

A bird can see water.

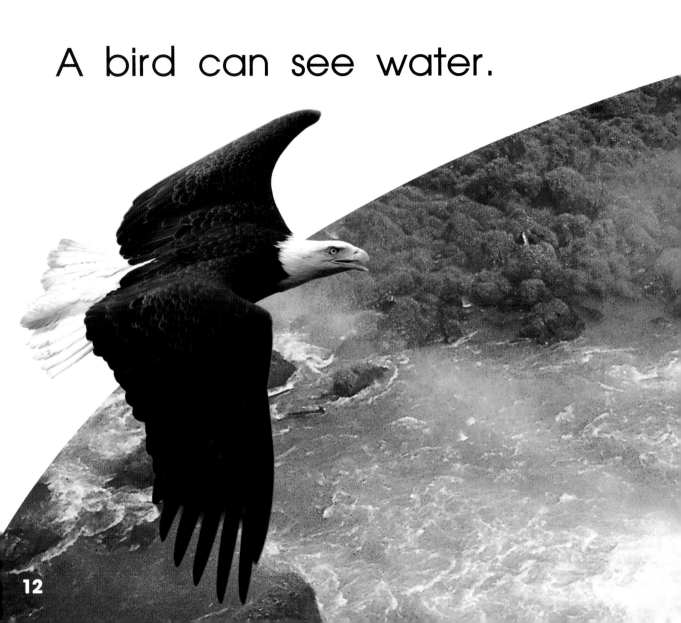

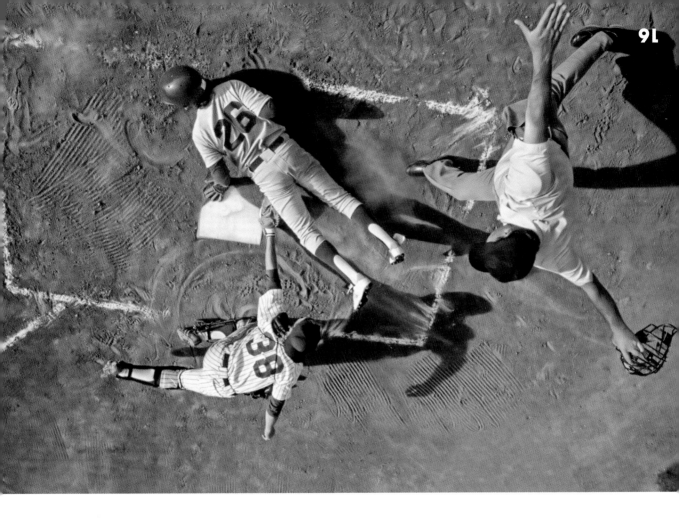

A bird can see people.

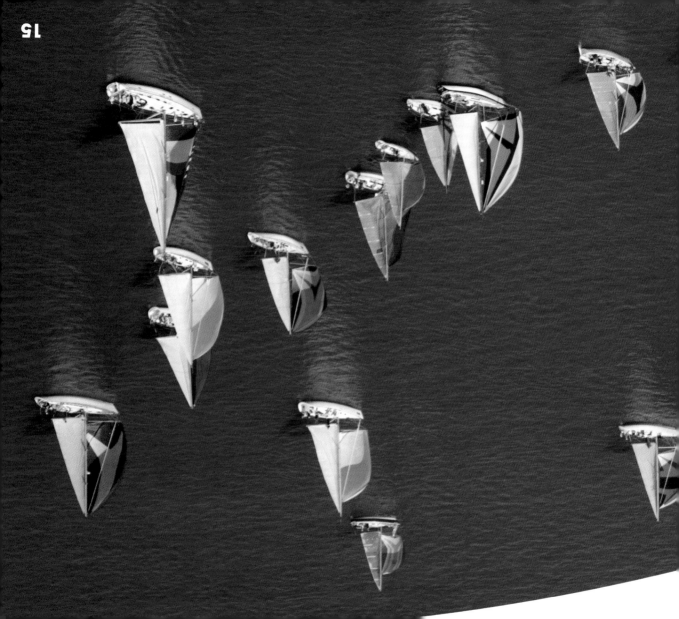

A bird can see boats.

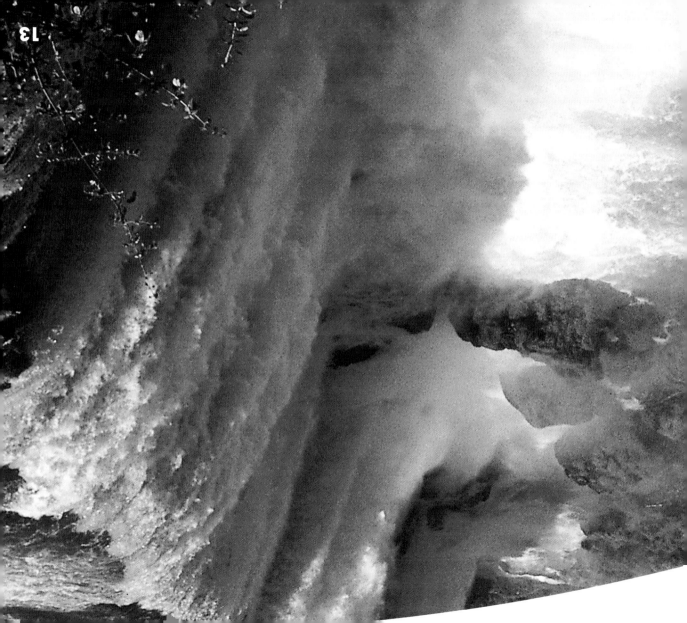